1989

CULTURAL AWARENESS IN THE HUMAN SERVICES

JAMES W. GREEN

University of Washington

With contributions by
Joseph Gallegos
Hideki A. Ishisaka
James W. Leigh
Nancy B. Miller
Calvin Y. Takagi
Theresa A. Valdez

Prentice-Hall, Inc., Englewood Cliffs, New Jersey 07632

Library of Congress Cataloging in Publication Data

Green, James W.
    Cultural awareness in the human services.

    (Prentice-Hall series in social work practice)
    Bibliography.
    Includes index.
        1. Social work with minorities.   I. Title.
II. Series.
HV3176.G73   362.8'4   81-15869
ISBN 0-13-195362-1   AACR2

Prentice-Hall Series in Social Work Practice
Neil Gilbert and Harry Specht, editors

> In the country of the blind,
> who are not as unobservant as they look,
> the one-eyed is not king, he is spectator.
>
> *Clifford Geertz*

Printed in the United States of America

10   9   8   7   6   5   4   3   2   1

Editorial/production supervision: Maureen Connelly
Cover design: Lee Cohen
Manufacturing buyer: John Hall

ISBN 0-13-195362-1

Prentice-Hall International, Inc., *London*
Prentice-Hall of Australia Pty. Limited, *Sydney*
Prentice-Hall of Canada, Ltd., *Toronto*
Prentice-Hall of India Private Limited, *New Delhi*
Prentice-Hall of Japan, Inc., *Tokyo*
Prentice-Hall of Southeast Asia Pte. Ltd., *Singapore*
Whitehall Books Limited, *Wellington, New Zealand*